YARN

Maitreyabandhu was born Ian Johnson in 1961 in Warwickshire. He initially trained as a nurse at the Walsgrave Hospital, Coventry, then went on to study fine art at Goldsmiths College, London. He started attending classes at the London Buddhist Centre (LBC) in 1986, and moved into a residential spiritual community above the LBC in 1987. He was ordained into the Triratna Buddhist Order in 1990 and given the name Maitreyabandhu.

Since then he has lived and worked at the LBC, teaching Buddhism and meditation. He has written three books on Buddhism, *Thicker than Blood: Friendship on the Buddhist Path* (2001), *Life with Full Attention: a Practical Course in Mindfulness* (2009) and *The Journey and the Guide: a Practical Course in Enlightenment* (2015) – all with Windhorse Publications. In 2010 he founded Poetry East, a new poetry venue exploring the relationship between spiritual life and poetry, and attracting many of the UK's foremost poets.

Maitreyabandhu has won many awards including the Keats-Shelley Prize, the Basil Bunting Award, the Geoffrey Dearmer Prize, the Ledbury Festival Competition, the Poetry Book and Pamphlet Competition, and the Iota Shots Award. He has published two collections, with Bloodaxe, *The Crumb Road* (2013), a Poetry Book Society Recommendation, and *Yarn* (2015).

MAITREYABANDHU

YARN

BLOODAXE BOOKS

ISBN: 978 1 78037 262 4

First published 2015 by
Bloodaxe Books Ltd
Eastburn
South Park
Hexham
Northumberland NE46 1BS

www.bloodaxebooks.com
For further information about Bloodaxe titles
please visit our website or write to
the above address for a catalogue.

Supported using public funding by
ARTS COUNCIL
ENGLAND

Cover design: Neil Astley & Pamela Robertson-Pearce.

Printed in Great Britain by Bell & Bain Limited, Glasgow, Scotland, on
acid-free paper sourced from mills with FSC chain of custody certification.

For Mimi Khalvati

ACKNOWLEDGEMENTS

Some of these poems, or earlier versions of them, were published in *Agenda, Ambit, Acumen, Dream Catcher, The Frogmore Papers, The Moth, The New Humanist, The North, Nutshell Magazine, Poem, The Poetry Review, The Rialto* and *Urthona*. I'm especially grateful to *Long Poem Magazine* for publishing earlier versions of 'The Cattle Farmer's Tale' and 'The Travellers from Orissa'.

'Four Men' and 'Settlement' were originally published in *Vita Brevis*, which won the Iota Shots Award (2012) and was a Poetry Book Society Pamphlet Choice (Spring 2013). An earlier version of 'Star Man' was published in *Poetry News* and in *The Poet's Quest for God*, ed. Oliver Brennan (Eyewear Publishing, 2015). An earlier version of 'Two Birds for Kabir' was published in *Hildegard: Visions and Inspiration*, an illustrated anthology published in limited edition by Wyvern Works (Rome, 2014).

I'm grateful to Shravasti Dhammika for his help with 'The Travellers from Orissa' and 'The Cattle Farmer's Tale' – both poems have been enriched by his Pali scholarship. I'd like to thank Carol Rumens, for her helpful comments on an earlier version of 'The Travellers from Orissa'. Thank you again to Vishvantara Julia Lewis for her unfailing encouragement. I am especially grateful to Mimi Khalvati, without whose help this collection would not have been possible. I'm greatly indebted to the Jerwood/Arvon and Escalator mentoring schemes, and to Arts Council England for their generous support.

CONTENTS

The Travellers from Orissa

Trace the knottings of your back
to another country,
already dreamlike – a table

laid out under apple trees,
putting on your coat
to walk into the rain.

These Days

The sun, at sunflower height,
makes the usual lanterns in the gorse,
        pine twigs bright
    as Golgi's pictures of the brain
    where nerves show up in silver nitrate

    and, although the breeze
is just enough to nod the Queen Anne's lace,
        nothing pleases –
    our human calculus precedes
    the given world: whatever seeds

    we plant will grow in time –
the error bred in the bone, the daily rancour
        of the mind,
    our clever ways to be unkind
    will spoil the morning, disinclined,

    as we so often are,
to watch this equal sunlight sculpt the day –
        a repertoire
    of olive green and cinnabar,
    from risen moon to evening star.

Sunday

Someone has kicked the ladders away
and nothing reassures –
the figure of light, the lover, the sailor
with his telescope...

Nothing resolves this absence
without cause, this blank – a crow
commanding something from a branch;
a scatter of woodpigeons.

Then later, when the sky comes back
with an evening mildness –
a squirrel's smoke-tail
following the arc of its leap.

Nietzsche's Sponge

Not to be estranged but more at home
in the comfort of my legs, their weight
and warmth, I pictured open summer sky
but stories I've told a thousand times before –

the one about success, the other aggrieved
(you'd think I'd tire, you'd think I'd give it up) –
erased the far horizon like Nietzsche's sponge.
I strained to see the Vajra Guru's face

or feel his love but he stayed between the rick
of thought and that other world where form
slips away to formlessness and shows us

perfected, as we are beyond ourselves –
the Greatly Precious One from Oḍḍiyāna,
the Lotus Born, the Yogi, and the King.

The Postulant

He felt himself to be the painful intersection
between two blissful worlds – a water splash
or knot of air. He'd closed his eyes on this world –
the sun just rising in the east, the fret of birds,
his frown from where two circles overlapped –
and where no flowers grew, his heaving breath
was chain-link or the figure of eight rotating.
When night fell, the space between two worlds
was all the shape he made, an empty dark without
moons or badgers while some piston pressure
or odd exertion was pushing the spheres apart
as if a great machine would move the aching stars.
What he thought to be himself he didn't know:
his pain was all that stopped the worlds unite.

The Cattle Farmer's Tale

He was standing in the middle of the yard
waiting for me to speak and it was this
that put me on my guard – his not pretending
to be meek or grateful to set me at my ease
and, funny thing, it stopped me in my tracks
so for a moment I stumbled on my words –

'You'll be wanting somewhere to lay your head
now they say the rains are sure to come.'
I led him to the house, laying down
the rule I always had for the likes of him:
two weeks maximum and keep away
from the calves and womenfolk. I called my wife
and would've waited but something made me fuss
with bowls and cups and busy myself with talking.

'Last year the cowshed was all but washed away,
the rain came down so hard, but now I'm ready
and can truly say "If you want to rain, rain-god,
then go ahead and rain!"' I liked the phrase
I'd found and liked to use it. He smiled at this
and seemed about to speak but then my wife
came in, firelight brightening up her face.

> *The rice is cooked,*
> *the milking's done,*
> *the grain is safely stowed,*
> *the rain can come*
> *and drum and drum...*

It was an old song, my father used to sing it
in that flat voice of his, this time of year.
The man sat very still and watched me sing.

Usually with the likes of him, homeless men
spending the night wheresoever they can,
under a tree or in a dirty shed, usually
they get to talking straight away like folk
who're starved of company – so the silence
made me wish I'd given him short shrift
and shown him to the gate.

                  'Thirty milkers,'
I said as I sat down, 'that's how many
cows I've got. I go over with the slops
and they come up to the fence as if they're friends –
yearlings and milch cows, heifers and breeding bulls.
I've level paddy fields with good embankments
and corn that's high enough to hide a crow!'
My voice was louder than I'd meant as if
I spoke to someone right across the room.
'If you've walked along the Mahi riverbank
you'll have seen the barns – my father left them –
good and strong as anyone's around.'

'My mind is fertile' he said, putting down
his cup. 'Wherever I look it might be fields
of wheat or well-ploughed irrigated land.'
He had a way of saying 'fertile', an accent
I couldn't place, but I could see he was
an educated man. I'd half a mind
he meant to lecture, so I jumped in quick
with what I had to say.

                  'I've men who'll pick
the flies away and light the smoky fires
to keep mosquitoes off. The fields I own
are ready for the rains, the cows are strong
and range about the meadows where they will.'
I left a gap for him to see the good of it.

'I have no need of shelter; my hut's unthatched
and all the household fires are out.' He looked
to where my wife stood like a frightened doe,
her eyes so wide and timid by the door.
I bade her fetch the kummasa and rice
but she waited like she might've disobeyed.
Well, I could see the game that we were playing –
a man on either side – so I waved her off,
then carried on to see where we would go.

'I've had my work cut out – trenches to dig,
rafters to mend with honest working men
as rare as hare's horn. Working's all there is
for those of us who have a house to feed –
the stakes are in, the ropes are firmly tied –
but you see the farm's my own; I'm lord
of all that I survey, so I can sit here
anytime I choose and talk to you like this.'

'My work's the Aryan Eightfold Way, my rest's
Nibbana's cave. I live on my awakening –
a cloud that might be gathered in and caught.
My home's the dust roads of this floating world;
my drink's the Law-rain falling on the ground;
my sons and daughters are the quickly growing
munja-grass and vines – so if you want to
rain, rain god, then go ahead and rain!'
He smiled at me to give my saying back.

'I've four good sons; you watch them coming in.
You've seen my wife, how obedient she is –
compliant and restrained, I never hear
a bad word said about her.'

'My mind is tamed,
compliant to my will. And love sits here –'
he pointed to his heart, then smiled again
to show me it was true. 'Once, like you,
I had a handsome wife, a son, fine lands,
a wealthy father – I left that all behind,
seeing it would end.

> *I built a raft of ropes and wood*
> *and tied it tight and made it trim,*
> *then set the sail to make it good*
> *and though the current bucked and skimmed,*
> *I landed on the further shore*
> *where there was sorrow nevermore.'*

He rocked slightly while he sang, his voice
so sweet and almost hidden in his breath.

I felt a lurching in my brain; I tried
to speak again and meant to shout him down
but something in his gaze – so frank, so true –
held me like a hunted deer. All at once,
like some great drum stretched tight across the world,
thunder shook the sky while lightning cast
his shadow massive on the wall and then
the rains came roaring on the roof as if
Namuchi's army were fighting to get in
with slings and arrows, lightning clubs and bolts.
I wrenched my gaze away and turned aside.

Suddenly I saw a figure in the doorway
all dressed in pelting rain – his face was grey,
a kind of whispered comfort came from him
and when he spoke his voice was soft and bubbling
in his throat:

Everyday I'll sing
the song of your delight.
Those with children win delight
and everyday they sing!

Everyday brings joy
in prosperous farm and cattle.
For the sake of keeping cattle
everyday brings joy!

Everyday brings peace
from gods of hearth and home.
With a wife who keeps the home,
everyday brings peace!

Everyday…

'There are two thoughts, Dhaniya,' –
the vagrant laid his hand upon my arm –
'one leads to suffering, the other to joy.
The first is yoked to yearning like a calf,
a suckling calf that's yoked unto his mother,
the other's like a shadow that never parts.
That intoxicated man whose main delight
is in family, wealth and cattle, death
comes and carries him off like a great flood
that sweeps away a sleeping village – sons
are no protection, nor father's land, nor wife.'

Something was holding all the water back.
I let it break. And rushing black and muddy
in the room, the torrent came and heaved
and seemed about to wash away the house
and drown us all but then it lifted me
into the Heaven of the Yearning Gods –

my body made of air and white as curds –
and there I seemed to linger like a star...

My wife returned with the dish of kummasa.
At first I didn't reckon what it meant
or where I sat or who this woman was
who bent beside my chair. I looked to where
the man had spoken from the open door
but all I saw were shawls of falling rain.
Then the vision fell away; the room
came back – I could recognise my things –
and I was home again inside my daily life.
I heard a voice that cried – it was my voice
in my mouth – 'What do you call this, woman?
Who asked for kummasa? Bring him the best,
for he is worthy of the choicest gifts;
this two-fingeredness is unbecoming.'
I saw a tear starting in her eye.
She looked afraid to hear me speak like that,
so I was sorry and went to go and help.

He stayed a month until the rain had stopped.
And while he stayed he'd come and teach us both
sitting quietly in this room, quietly talking.
Every night my wife would cook her finest –
sukaramamsa and jujube fruit, milk-rice,
gavapana mixed with honey and palm sugar,
galub jamun – her eyes had tears of joy.
But finally he left. We watched him go,
half-hoping he'd turn back. We waited while
his figure disappeared... sometimes I think
that afternoon, it was us who disappeared.
For days I couldn't settle to my work –
the farm was scant and empty while the room
seemed water-lit, like the inside of a bridge.

I'd sit and stare and try to catch his shadow
grow tall again and dance across the wall.
But even now I struggle to describe him –
was he tall or short? I can hear his voice,
sometimes, and now and then I see his face
which seems the face of everyone I know.

Dhikr

Once more the breeze blew mild among the poplar trees
and made a speech of waverings and feints that woke

the brotherhood who dreamt the same and equal dream:
a flight of stairs on which disciples went, the Teacher

slowly dying on the floor. He played and sang
a slowly-climbing song, his voice now thin and reedy.

The oldest joined in the refrain while others wept.
And as they looked he seemed to change – his hair grew rich,

his voice thickened, till amid that sorrow song,
in hushed amazement, a new devotee said 'Bhante,

when you sing you seem much younger with each verse.'
'Auspicious to see your Teacher thus!' came the reply.

Asaṅga

When Asaṅga came down from his mountain cave –
twelve years that had achieved nothing –
he saw a dog, a miserable thing, abandoned,
whipped, with a suppurating sore that crawled
with maggots and blowflies. He knelt
and with his tongue he moved the maggots one by one
to a lump of his own flesh that he had cut away.
And suddenly Maitreya stood before him, saying

I have been with you all this time.
Everyday I came to your cave among the snows.
Carry me on your shoulders to the marketplace
and you will see how, unless the eye of faith
has opened, I will pass unnoticed there.

They went among the cabbages and chickpeas
and no one noticed Maitreya in his majesty,
the bent old monk or the dog that trotted by his side.

Ryōkan

Zazen every morning,
the way the cuckoo sings,
the seasons at their turning,
he preferred repeated things

like walking in the evening
or bathing at the spring,
the moon already rising,
he preferred repeated things:

old books and all their learning,
the temple bell, its ring –
how *everything* is burning –
he preferred repeated things.

from The Daybook of Li Shu Tong

Sometimes when it's still, a single howl of wind will curl around the temple yard and shake the cherry tree. You can hear it coming, louder, then still louder from beyond the Southern Ridge. It'll flip your robe and blow the water off your bucket! Then something draws it further off; you can see it – blue-grey scales edged with gold – a dragon-wind lifting bamboo mats and carrying a few red maple leaves right up to where the Buddha sits.

*

My duty is to clear the urine pits. The pits are filled with pine needles that have been dried out in the sun (we throw away the broken twigs and pine cones). First we dig the sopping needles out. The smell flies up with many angry bees. Urine spatters up your legs – you're allowed that day not to wear your robes. The stinking mud has to be scooped out and barrowed off, leaving an acrid trail. After digging out and raking over, the warm needles that have blonded in the sun have to be layered in and patted down, the stones replaced around them – white uneven stones to mark the place you stand.

*

Today we cleared the Image Hall again. We made a chain that snaked across the courtyard and passed out the mats and zafus – all this in silence – the Master passing from the front.. The mats were thrown over a branch and beaten with a stick. Then the Image Hall was swept and swept again – a line of us reversing on our knees, polishing the floor. All the doors and windows were thrown open to let the spring breeze in. By evening puja, everything was back, the mats and folded blankets. But when we got inside, we had to search for the zafus we preferred while the Master grinned and watched us bending down and turning. I ended up with one blanket less but with the Master already sitting, I had to stop. I feared the cold but then, in front of me, the farm boy's feet. He was holding out a blanket and smiling in my face so hard I had to lower my eyes.

*

I found out it is Dajian who walks so noisily when he goes out of the Image Hall, hitting his heals then smacking down his soles. I take him aside, 'You walk like a farm boy' I say, but he replies 'My parents were very poor. They didn't teach me how to be quiet, could you show me please?' I say 'There's nothing to show' but he insists, so we go into the Image Hall – the Buddhas smiling down and watching – and slowly, very quietly from one end to the other, I walk across the floor. He tries and gets it right first time, then unaccountably starts to giggle, which sets me off – the two of us holding each other up as our laughter peals around the room.

Four Men

They could be painted on a commemorative plate,
sitting at a table in a variety of poses –
taking bread, holding a cup, and so forth…

The plate might be telling stories of Brotherhood
or Temperance: four men pictured in double scale –
the veranda and dark rooms leading off it

fitting around them as if they had become giants.
The woodpile by the path – sawn pine logs
stacked at right angles, tier on tier – suggests

New Hampshire or Vermont, but they are in Spain
and the ground is thick with needles. The folds
and creases of their robes evoke the *Schöne Stil*

of International Gothic whose figures move
more easily in space, with animals, scrupulously
depicted plants, and the first real sky we know.

The Marker

He was snapping shut his book when he saw,
say, twenty pages on, another marker,
not the one he'd used and slipped between
the leaves but a band of silk with fancy tassels
and words embroidered round the edge in language
he couldn't read. Someone had gone ahead
and looked into the future, so he couldn't
be alone – not with lamplight burning low
and wind rattling the windows. He listened
for someone's breath, their footfall on the stair,
and he couldn't sleep that night for thinking
what it meant and what she knew, this lady
(he thought she'd be a lady) who read the story
further on and left him deeper in the shade.

The Dolphin

Again it swims back into view,
        the dolphin of depression,
grey-eyed, grey and jumping through
        the burning hoops of passion,

then diving to a colder district –
        shadow, a wheel of shadow –
where eels and multicoloured fish,
        the hopes for my tomorrow,

'I won't be jealous any more,
        I'll concentrate…' all this
(and love of course, the bedroom door
        shut tight) 'makes much amiss'

as another poet said.
        A wasteful sun comes out
and daylight sparks the coral bed;
        the quivering waterspout,

a rippling stalk that holds aloft
        the beach-ball of delight
to whoops and cheers, is tempest-tossed
        and falls, the show is blighted

and again it swims back into view,
        the dolphin of depression –
the grin is false, the song untrue,
        the tricks are out of fashion.

New Year's Eve, Sydney

After the fireworks above the bridge – bouquets
erupting in reverse in the black water of the harbour,
gun–echoes, cannon–echoes, claps and long fizzes

resounding off apartment blocks, children writing
Happy New Year in sparkler on the near dark, adults
tipping champagne into unstable plastic cups, teenagers

wearing pulsating blue light-jewellery while nearby
a party starts up in the orangey lit aquarium of a kitchen –
after we'd walked up the hill with blankets,

then back again among dead-eyed wooden bungalows
(and I was so unhappy because that would be the year
I'd lose you), we saw a man walking his dog

stop in the neon pool of a streetlight, look up at the sky
and there on the slung telephone wire, a kookaburra
like some great quiet soul come to watch over us:

*Oh procrastinating one, devoting yourself to the useless
doings of this life – mistaken indeed would your purpose
now be if you returned empty-handed from this life!*

Star Man

He saw a blue light entering his heart
coming from a man he couldn't see
but knew was standing in the stars above
the playing field behind the neighbour's house.
The light came like a curl of candle smoke
and lit an apple tree inside his head
where once he'd built a den and brought flowers
in a coronation mug without its handle.
He could see the usual things – the laurel hedge,
the path that marked the border of his world –
but no river murmured powerful thoughts,
no wind of meaning blew among the stars,
no nature's heart beat full against his own,
just apple branches illumined in the dark.

The World of Senses

I yearn for this much-prized, painful love –
his smile, the way he moves his hips
when he cuts a loaf or stirs a soup
or my chest against his back – this love
that quietly lifts away when he falls asleep.

I yearn for this much-desired success –
vaulting ambition, rapt applause
as I bend to take my seat, awards
received in feigned surprise – success
that barely adds a farthing to my store.

But I never yearn for you, the Lotus Born –
frown and smile and trident staff,
illumined image through which I'd pass
beyond this world of senses, borne
across the waters, safely, by your raft.

The Stain

In that other now of past-in-present,
a flagstone path runs beside
the playing field dotted as before
with buttercups and daisies.

The path leads to a classroom
where an angel with doily wings
and white pipe cleaner arms
smiles and holds a shepherd's crook.

But then the path gives way –
a shoal of sugarpaper fish
turn together while a grass stain
blooms across your shirt.

Pastoral

*There is no excellent beauty that hath not
some strangeness in the proportion.*

FRANCIS BACON

The man wearing Elizabethan dress
(it is 1825) is either asleep
in his nook, propped up on his bolster
of cornflowers and ivy hearts, or scanning
the open pages of a book – ankles
crossed and quite at ease with the moon
in the ivory-carved, sepia-tinted half-dark
of Samuel Palmer's half-visionary drawing
The Valley Thick with Corn – 'nature is much
improved by being taken into the soul.'

Umber lines that 'cannot be got too black',
elucidate the sheaves while distant sheep
drink a puddle-mirror buoyed up in the grass.
The corn ears in the foreground, an abnormal
swollen crop, are our Harvest Sunday loaves.
'We are not troubled (wrote the painter)
by aerial perspective in the valley of vision' –
a tiny farm cart sauntering up a track,
the church spire just beyond it, ample trees
of mother love to keep the nightmare back.

The Pavilion

a birthday poem

What was it? 'We all come weeping here
with piteous cries and pipped alarm calls...'
This pair of coots, for instance, near

the café terrace, the pitch and fall
of minor waters, the weedy nest
they've built and must rebuild, all

the sticks they've had to find and rest
against each other to make this home
for five quickly growing guests

who must be fed.
                    The pass of Hakone
'bright this snowy morning' took Bashō
to the city of Nagoya – wind-moan,

the lake 'chaste with flowers of snow' –
to be the guest of honour at a
snow party, a crowded window

where they watched the snowflakes gather
after the tea ritual; then, old
before his time, on a litter

to Ueno – bamboo groves,
children the same height as the barley,
a storm bird's cry among the clouds –

already ill, he made the journey,
his final journey home in June.
There he wrote, on hearing Jutei,

his dead son's wife, had died so soon
'Don't think your life didn't matter' –
summer insects, an autumn moon,

snow at Irago.
                        The sound of laughter
brings me back. The coots are still
busy while the waiters clatter

dirty plates. Invisible
to them, cradling morning coffee
I stare at age: unthinkable

sad time…I turn to Bashō's *sabi*
to find solace in a solitariness
akin to no-mind and poetry –

a cuckoo in Kyoto, a nest
of coots – their watchful, nervy heads –
this curious sense of tragic lightness,
a shallow river and a sandy bed.

3rd June 2014

Seasonal Prayer

This knotted garland of success,
daffodils and crocuses
that grow in every council park –
nature's exclamation marks –
in such deluding fantasy,
may the Buddhas bear with me.

This stubborn feeling of despair,
snow-sleet in the freezing air
that blows across a mountain lake
and makes its darkness concentrate:
in such a sickness of self-pity,
may the Buddhas bear with me.

Two Birds for Kabir

A tree was growing in the sky
on which two birds were darkly perched.
The air was blond; the earth was grey.
The tree was silver, like a birch.

The tree was like a winter tree –
no leaves were gathered round the base
nor did it bow in sympathy
to make a shrine or sheltered place.

One bird was on a higher bough.
She watched the other eat the fruit
that, plump within a holy Now,
grew as an everlasting truth.

And as she ate, the juice that dripped
was falling into empty space
in shining devanagari script
like hot tears on a *chela's* face

or beads from a broken rosary.
And so they perched forever there –
two birds upon a rootless tree,
one eating, one in silent prayer.

The Travellers from Orissa

Tapussa said the oxen stood stock-still
and wouldn't budge although we slapped their haunches,
dragged their stubborn necks; he said they stood
and swung their heads and looked around themselves
as if a tiger might be roaming. Tapussa
said all the birds stopped singing and the day
was still but Tapussa's head was full of yarns –
he'd spin a story time and time again,
it got more fantastical each time he did
although he'd bridle if you dared to tell him.
I'd long got used to all his talk – the ox,
the birds, the unearthly light making us gape
and our neck-hairs bristle. Every time he'd add
another sight: the Four Great Kings arriving
with a magic bowl; a canopy of jewels;
a friendly snake wrapped round and round a prince!
But it's true we stopped. And it's true the day was still.

We left the boy with the cart and market grain,
the oxen tethered-up, their sandy hides
spotted with light. The sun was going down;
it was afternoon, it shone into the trees.
I can see the forest edges even now –
the light in narrow bands between the trunks,
màluvà creepers and red simbali flowers.
We found a path; it was rough and hard to tread
with prickly bushes catching on our clothes
and leaves high up like shields and warrior spears.
We found a level clearing in the wood,
a delightful spot! with kusha grass growing
under trees and the rushing sound of water.
Tapussa said that when we saw the Master
I nearly ran, as if he'd been a ghost

or a spirit of the dead, but why should I?
I'm not a fool.

        He was thin, I remember that,
and dirty! like a street boy thick with mud.
Tapussa jumped in with all the usual questions –
what dhamma do you teach and what's your caste?
He'd shake his head and sigh each time the Master
answered but I knew he didn't understand.
The Master spoke in a funny way with gaps
between the words as if he'd just been woken
from a dream. Tapussa kept on asking
foolish questions so I shut my mouth
and went to get some food. I brought the Master
barley gruel and madhupinda – his smile,
I shan't forget, was like gazing at the sea.

*

The sun had set but the evening sky was bright
when we got back to the cart. The journey
home was just the same as the journey out,
or so I've come to think: bumps and ridges,
the farm-boy's sullen face. One thing I do
remember – don't ask why – was a heron
standing at the edge of a scrubby pond.
I'd been sleeping in my seat and when I woke
my neck was stiff. I shifted up and looked.
I don't know what it was about the bird,
he seemed so old and sore and so intent
on that small meal that he was fishing for.

Kurangi, my wife, was standing at the door
when I got home with the boys around her skirts
and the bullock rigged and ready for the fields.
We married when we were young and got along
much easier than most. She often laughed

when Tapussa spoke, which of course he didn't like.
He grew impatient with my quiet – he'd call round
late at night when the boys were long in bed.
One time he'd been with the village lads
telling tales, all kinds of things – marvels
and ghostly visitations, I don't know what –
well, he must have felt ashamed because he came
and got me out of bed so we could talk.
I wouldn't speak at first but he looked so hurt
I told him all I remembered of the day –
how we'd seen the Master under a peepal tree,
the way he looked and smiled, the journey home.
I was surprised by what I had to say.
Tapussa was quiet and we stood there in the dark.

One time I told Kurangi. She'd been pestering
for days, so I talked about it straight, how I'd laughed
and touched the Master's arm, kissed his feet,
then wept when it was time to leave. After that
I'd catch her looking at me strange, so I knew
to keep it to myself.

                I thought it over
in the fields which was where I was happy most,
standing behind the plough with birds riding
on the bullock's back, the sun riding
the water's edge and the air thick with midges.
That's when it would all come back, not often
and never when I tried to get it straight –
once when I was lifting up my youngest boy
and once when the sun was low behind the trees.
When the feeling came, it hurt around my heart
and made me shake and tremble. I'd have to stop.
The boys would cluster round and start to cry,
throwing down their sticks. Then whatever it was
would lift and I'd want to jump for joy. I'd clap

the bullock's back then give the boys a ride,
or I'd fold my hands and fall down in the dust.

*

Tapussa started wearing homespun stained
with clay; he attracted a little following –
they came to ask him what he thought and how
the crops would fare and who would make a bride.
He stopped talking to me about that time.
He'd pretend he didn't see me when I passed.
I kept my thinking to myself but Kurangi
would complain and want to take it up,
the rumours he'd been spreading – I'd shake my head
and she'd relent and go outside to work.
Sometimes we'd laugh and be like kids again;
we'd do impersonations of his ways –
his nodding head, how he held his finger up
each time he spoke to emphasise each word.
Tapussa said the Master sent a deva
to teach him dhamma while he slept; he said
he heard a voice inside a tree or speaking
from a rock – he'd stop and seem to listen!

Then he got ill…oh, ten years ago at least,
and near the end his wife asked me to come.
She was waiting at the door when I arrived.
She asked about the boys – how grown up
they were and tall. The room inside was dark
and I could smell the nishigandha flowers.
Tapussa was on his back all dressed in white
and someone had hung a chain of marigolds
around his neck as if he was already dead
and living with the Gods of the Thirty Three.
We didn't speak but I knew what he would have said.

Then Kurangi died. She'd not been herself for weeks –
she kept clutching her side and screwing up
her face but when I asked her what was wrong
she'd shrug it off and tell me it was nothing.
Then once I heard her shouting at the boys.
The youngest had broken something or knocked a dish
of lentils on the ground – he was always clumsy –
and when I came she was leaning on the door.
I'd never heard her scream like that before.
Next day I met them running from the house
telling me to come home straight away.
I found her in bed already cold and curled up
on her side as if having pleasant dreams.

                              *

Occasionally a merchant would turn up
and tell a story: what the Master said
at such-a-place, the way he'd talk, how he'd treat
a Brahmin's son. I'd go along and listen
with the rest but it didn't make much sense.
When I tried to remember when we met,
it was like it happened to someone else, it seemed
so long ago. So when we heard the news
that he was three days' walk away with a band
of hangers-on, I nearly didn't go,
but Meghiya, my youngest son, got so excited
he put my walking stick into my hand
and almost pushed me out the door, despite
my aches and troubles. We met all kinds of folk
from local towns; I'd stop and tell the story
once again but Meghiya would complain
and say we must keep going. I did my best.
I went about as fast as I could manage.
Paddy fields and coconut trees and scrub
are all I can remember of the journey
except perhaps the kikā's raucous call –
such lovely wings and such an awful cry.

How good it was to be among the noise!
I felt like I was twenty seasons younger –
stalls laid out, women carrying pots,
bullock carts and tethered buffalo.
Hungry crows were waiting on the roofs
to steal away a scrap and there were children
playing games and getting under my feet.
I would have stopped to ask about the price
of madulaja but Meghiya took me sternly
by the elbow among the jostling crowd.
When we got to the ambavana, among
the banyan trees, we couldn't hear the things
the Master said for all the buzz of talk.
Meghiya kept on telling them to shush,
turning sharply round, pressing his finger
to his lips while young men blocked my view.
Eventually we turned our steps back home,
Meghiya, dejected, straggling behind.
We'd not got far beyond the hawkers' cry,
the smoke and cooking smells, when there he was,
the Master! walking a little way ahead
with a motley crew of sadhus and disciples.
I knew him by the way he moved – slow
and even like an elephant or tiger.
Meghiya didn't notice him at first
but I said 'Master' before I knew I spoke
(I'd never used the word before). He turned
and said my name – my name! – *Bhallika* he said,
so soft, I felt ashamed. I wept so hard
I thought my ribs would break. He said 'Good',
then carried on his way.

*

　　　　　As a boy,
Meghiya had always been the talkative one.
He'd follow me around asking questions,
then ask 'Why?' each time I tried to answer.

Kurangi used to say, 'If you'd only
put the effort you put into your tongue
into your chores, we might get something done!'
Well, that day we walked in silence home,
Meghiya looking sidelong with a question
written on his face. I tried to talk
of other things – some paddy fields we passed,
a kukutthaka starting up – *hoo popo!* –
but he saw what I was doing and wouldn't speak.
I'd kept the secret feeling to myself
ever since that day I'd told Kurangi,
knowing I'd not be understood and doubting
if I would be now, but I was overawed,
meeting the Master and weary from the road,
so I opened up my heart, trusting to the Gods.

Everything was true about the place, I said –
the forest grove, the food I went and fetched –
but after we had eaten and after Tapussa
had gone through all his questions once again
and hardly listened and had no more to say,
the Master said – I remember every word,
I've kept them with me all this time – he said
'Listen my friends! There is a thorn buried
in the heart of man. And for this thorn
they suffer here and now and in the future.
I have found that thorn and plucked it out
and for me the mass of suffering is no more.'
Tapussa jumped in saying 'Yes but – yes but –',
I could have struck him and quickly said his name
but the Lord, for so he seemed to me just then,
looked at him with such a heart of love,
I couldn't speak. And then a wonder came
and troubled me and worked within my soul
as if I'd rise and shout and stamp my feet
but then I saw Kurangi's face, the boys,

46

the village fields I'd always known – how could I
leave and walk the Triple World with him?
My heart was like a netted fish thrown up
upon a dusty bank and thrashing wildly
but the Master, the Happily Attained,
Guide Unsurpassed of Men to be Tamed,
the Blessèd One, Richly Endowed – he seemed
to search inside my heart and urge it forward.

I didn't follow the Blessèd One that day.
I left with Tapussa, as I said, and walked
back into my life and tried to take it up,
the way I'd always lived. Only Kurangi
knew that something deep inside had changed.
And soon I found how little I could say.
And soon I gave up trying, even with her.
Tapussa hadn't understood. He'd turned
the whole thing upside-down and made it all
about himself and how he stood and what
he had to say…I'd kept a stubborn silence.
And though I've loved my children one and all,
Meghiya best perhaps, and though my life's
been blessed – I won't complain – I knew as I
climbed inside the cart, the sky still bright
above my head and half the journey done,
I knew that day that I'd betrayed my life.

*

Now I'm old. I don't know how old, my mother
was never clear about that sort of thing.
She used to say, 'You're the same age as your nose
and just a few years older than your teeth' –
I'm sure that I'm the oldest in the village.
Nowadays youngsters come to ask me questions
or talk about their fears. I listen or say
a word or two, then ask them not to worry.

They mostly want to hear about the Master
although they've heard it umpteen times before.
I usually protest, but if they insist
or if they're young, I add the things Tapussa
would have said – the snake, the Four Great Kings,
the crystal bowl of light. I like to watch
their faces, how they gasp and put their hands up
to their mouths and stare at me in wonder.
I have to be careful though: if I miss something out
they stop me and say I haven't got it right!

Meghiya left that day we met the Master.
I had to let him although it broke my heart.
Now his wife looks after me, she's good
and quiet, and soon she'll bring me yàgu
before I go to bed. The monsoon rains
have started early, drumming on the roof
like a herd of angry goats or an army
from the west; it's almost like I'm living
in the sea, I might be a darting shoal
of fish, my mind seems full of roving eyes!
At times like this I think I hear Tapussa
preaching dhamma to the village lads
or Kurangi singing while she bathes the boys –
I hear their squeals coming through the night.
And sometimes when I'm about to fall asleep
I hear the Master calling out my name
over and over – *Bhallika!* – *Bhallika!* – quietly
between the drops. I know it's just my mind
playing tricks, but I listen nonetheless.

April Elegies

i.m Mahananda/Andrew Andrzej Serafinski
21st June 1947 – 2nd April 2009

Your death blurs with other
deaths this April morning
outside the crematorium
stooping to look at wreaths

Name-giving

When I gave you your name you wept aloud.
I'd made a path, a kind of sacred floor
winding under pale grey cirrus cloud,
last cherry leaves, a final sycamore –

a double row of candles leading where
I said you'd have to die: The Tiger's Cave.
I'd gone along before to tidy and prepare
the things you'd need to take beyond the grave.

You had no shortage of uproar and history –
Poland and the war both played their part
that early evening – but you followed me

as I'd asked into the kindly English dark
to the place I'd garlanded, as if in jubilee,
the Bodhisattva's brow, the Buddha's marks.

Tumbalalaika

I saw a blackbird in the restaurant garden
on the day after you died –
he was busy in the light that seemed too bright,

too much like summer. You won't be coming back
as he has, year after year.
There'll be no more Yiddish songs for us to sing –

Tumbala, tumbala, tumbalalaika – no faces pulled
in a stuffy room. Your love
of chicory and the backs of buildings, the way

you used felt-tips – all that's in question now
along with wood smoke
hazy in the park and the nervy crowns of tulips.

I hold up your shirts, try on your gloves, ask
if I can keep the figure
of a saint standing on an inlaid wooden box

and your watch – the split across the strap
where the buckle went
still marking the size of your wrist.

Souls

I don't believe that souls are turned to birds.
Watch them on the lawn, the blackbirds stab
            the muddy grass for worms.

I don't believe that souls transform to deer
that track us from a wood, remembering
            their former human forms.

I don't believe that when the trumpet sounds,
the soul is given back its mortal flesh
            as brightly burning coals.

I don't believe the soul migrates and wears
a different body with each life or like
            a water drop dissolves.

They say we each live on in the gestures
of a child, but that doesn't count for you
            – no father to a son –

so what can I conclude on your departure?
that nothing came of it, with everything,
            everything undone?

Two Drawings

In the first, two figures, simply drawn –
charcoal figures without mouth or eyes
standing in the bottom right-hand corner,
a few strokes each – both have a frugal suitcase,
a smudge of grey, accusing at their feet.

The cobblestones are roughly sketched on which
the many couples with their cases meet,
each alike, in hats and coats, who gather
in a kind of civic space. But now a train
has shuffled in with heavy gouts of smoke

and rows of trucks are entering the drawing.
Snow blows round the cases standing there.
(These two, I think, must be his grandparents.)
A bell is rung. Train-smoke blots the picture.
Then a second sketch appears in present tense:

a wooden flight of stairs leads to a cellar
down which a figure steps. No ghosts, no rats –
his legs are fading as he moves. He meets
himself floating face-up in a rancid bath:
his genitals are drawn with four quick marks.

Zofia

You had to find your way without breathing
and you did – you walked, surprised how easy
now it was to leave the world behind.
But then the usual torments came: you'd find
your mother again, stepping off the boat,
a handbag with its handle worn or broken,
no shoes, no coat, no language she could speak
and that was where it started – London and peace,
peace after war, but not, you said, for her.
You had to listen to each recounted horror:
the agreed-on vase of flowers left in a window,
a sign that it was safe and no Gestapo
searched the house – but how this time the plan
went wrong and fear too big to understand
entered every life.

                   You stepped inside
my dream to tell me with a kind of pride,
your words a muddled rush, how death had come,
how foolish all your fears had been and wrong –
a song you stumbled through on your accordion –
how everything made sense, the fumbled facts,
your father's bible, the burning books and maps,
the Camps; even the European stain
found its settled place. There was no pain
in your voice, nothing like a cry or moan –
you were still the social man I'd known,
warm and garrulous in company.
You told me all of this and then embraced me.

Today I had to cycle to the street
by Primrose Hill where one damp night MacNeice
lay listening to the cutting down of trees,

clearing the hill's crest for light artillery –
the view prepared, searchlights probing heaven
for the bacilli of war. But that was then –
your 'then' still seems to me a 'now'. Your plan
when you got back from China and Xi'an
where you'd seen the terracotta soldiers
facing east to guard the old Qin Emperor
was to concentrate on 'the inward journey'
but not as far as this...

                I have your house key
so I lock my bike and open up your flat –
the camel rug, the piles of books and knick-knacks,
your shadow puppet, a dozen Chinese lamps,
the garden over-planted with exuberance.
I walk from room to room, opening doors,
babbling about tiling and parquet floors.
The estate agent suggests a change of décor
as April flickers sunlight on your desk –
the final envelope, the scrawled address
you started, then put aside in your distress.
She asks about the bathroom and the loo,
a better boiler, which carpets to renew,
which curtains. She's professional and nice:
we talk about the market and the asking price.

Birches in Sweden

What was the name of that lane
running next to Dillons
where I rode a Chopper bike?

Bear Lane? Doctors Lane?
It ran beyond the scrumping orchard
up to the building site

where we jumped on sandhills
and ran along planks
at the side of Station Road.

You've been out of the body so long
I can't imagine you –
though you'd have photographed

the signposts and barns.
I'd have talked about silver birches,
the ones behind our house –

drips of white paint
against the sky; you'd have met
someone whose grandfather

was in the Reich
or whose mother didn't survive.
There'd be something to weep about.

Den stora gåtan
The Great Enigma

After we had walked beyond the boats, above the dance ships
and the docked cruise liner, we found our way past the hospital
and stood opposite the block where Tomas Tranströmer lives.
We cupped our faces to the glass – stairs, a bookcase, a propped
bicycle – while above, in one of the apartments, he played
piano with his good hand, a line from Schubert, say, with
Schubert's that-was-long-ago sadness. In the garden nearby,
between two hunched-over wooden houses, dusty flowers,
which might have been cowslips or Swedish cowslips anyway,
grew in the not very well-tended borders. We could see the
sea. A bench ran round a sycamore where the poet might have
remembered snow painting over his footsteps – each leaf a
little shout of green. 'Hard to think we're in the city,' I said,
the tree crowning it all like a pause between traffic or the time
there wasn't any News. I took out my copy of Tranströmer
and, opening it at random, angled the pages so you could see:

*The night after the accident I dreamt of a pock-marked man
who walked through the alleys singing*

but now you're in the side ward, I'm ringing round your friends
and it's already too late. Someone's mopping a corridor. A few
of us go to a garage for sandwiches and crisps after I've stroked
your arm and told you 'I don't know…' The leaves barely
moved. The garden sloped and there were wooden steps leading
down to the harbour and the dockside cafés.

Five Years On

Five years on in blossom time
        your voice is coming back;
when all I thought you'd left behind
        were *things*, a broken watchstrap,
I find you talk to me in rhyme,
five years on in blossom time!

But five years on is five years dead
        so this can't be your voice
saying things you might have said –
        making a wiser choice
from twists and turnings up ahead,
five years on and five years dead.

His Funeral

What seems so strange now is I don't recall
your body in the open coffin, the men
in pinstripes, the polished brass of funeral.
Oh, I remember it all right – as when

we fall out of the usual etiquette
of death, when something has to give and jokes
are permissible again with cigarettes
while another April settles and evening cloaks,

in part, the failing-feeling we had to share.
But that's another kind of memory,
where you have to coax your mind, repair
the day in thought, tell yourself the story

from the start, then listen out for echoes.
The pulling of long faces had to end.
We dried our eyes. Unlike you, I suppose,
to be so quiet in a room so full of friends.

The Pianist's Name

The blackbirds have come back
to mark your absence. They build
in the wisteria, rebuild their mossy nest –

the male perched on the chimneypot
again, the female bringing worms.
I've still got your Post-it slipped

inside my Filofax with the directions
to your house in your flamboyant
saw-tooth script, the R and L

underlined for emphasis. I wish
you'd been given a few more years
after your mother died, after –

what was her name? – the pianist
who lived in your mother's block –
Natalia Karpf – played her final polonaise.

Unruly Times

Ten years later I read the book you gave me,
Unruly Times, about how Wordsworth kept pigs
and grew green beans and how Coleridge
was seen 'powdered' in London, so they knew,

the Wordsworths, that the argument no longer
rankled the big talker. On the flyleaf you wrote
thanks and love from your own unruly times,
big talker yourself and no stranger to dejection.

The magnolia must be blossoming again, white
between the streetlight and the car I walked
your friend back to, after the agony was done.

It was after Coleridge died that Wordsworth wrote
'Although I've hardly seen him these last years,
his mind, to me, has been habitually present.'

Historia

'Benek and I had an agreement that whoever came home first
would put a little flowerpot in the window, but the day
I was arrested I saw everything as if I was in a dream.
I turned into the road and at the corner there was a man
dressed in a black leather jacket and high boots
and I knew it was the Gestapo. I looked up at the house
but there was no flowerpot and yet I carried on to the staircase.
There was another man in boots in the entrance hall.
By now it was too late to turn back. I went up to the first floor
and put the key into the lock but the door was opened
by someone inside who addressed me as 'Frau Heilmann'
(Benek's surname) and I protested I was Frau Doblewska,
showing him my papers. But as I came into the room
I saw them all lying on the floor, including two or three
Jewish cousins who were visiting from the labour camp
and the son and daughter of the house. On a little stool,
sitting in the middle of the room, was a Gestapo man
with a revolver in his hand. Later it emerged that they had not
come to fetch me, Benek or any Jews, they had come
to arrest the householders who worked in the Underground.
But, unaware of this situation, I started to apologise
to the landlady for the misfortune we were bringing on the house.
She tried to wink to me to get me to stop talking.
We were then moved to the headquarters of the Gestapo
(Pomorska St?). There the others were tortured
but I was only measured. My head dimensions did not
agree with their Aryan theories of the Jewish race.
Then I was questioned – they wanted to know where
we had obtained false identity papers. I kept giving
evasive answers. He threatened to break my head open
with the typewriter and he burnt my dress twice
with his cigarette. I gave him a false address. He said
if it turned out to be the wrong one, he would get me.'

I buy a coffee at the little kiosk outside the Tube
and read from your *Historia* ('to learn by inquiry').
Squirrels chase each other across the park and now
that April gives way to May, the tulips have gone
and the cherry blossom. People lie or sit and talk
while the plane trees thicken. 'She sailed from Gdansk
and disembarked a few days later at the Tower of London.'
I see I've got the details wrong: she was wearing
wooden shoes, a coat made from a Red Cross army blanket
and had carried her hand-sewn cloth bag all the way
from Auschwitz. She never saw Benek again
(her first husband): 'I heard from various people he'd been shot.'
She met your father on that first day in London.
Two boys cycle past without holding the handlebars –
children and pigeons released from history's weight.
I've finally got your mother's story straight.

Colwall

Tired and still inside my London head,
   I walked up Oyster Hill
when suddenly and poet-like, a trill
      high above me,
   sounded as sharp and clear
as any hedge- or lane-lover might hear,

Hardy say, still in his time-torn prime –
   as if the very branch
was singing to the sky and no mischance
      could make England
   less than a green design
in summer weather. I should have banished mine.

These watercolour clouds and swabs of blue,
   this robin – I see him now –
can't assuage us for the world we know,
      your mother's war,
   I should have thought of you...
The world has grown too simple and too true.

The Private Ordination

I said your name and told you what it meant –
how your life had struggled to that point,
what you'd had to suffer, the darkest times
with demons, wrestled, wrestled without relent.

You wept to hear your name aloud, your name
to tell us who you really were: the same
and yet transformed, *Mahananda*, waiting
all that time, despite the reach of shame –

the dreams you told your psychoanalyst,
rages at your mother – despite all this
(eggs and china thrown to make her *hear*),
I knew your name should end with 'happiness'.

But more than that was *Maha*, meaning 'great',
'abundant', 'strong', the majesty and weight,
but what I emphasised was 'big', big
as your voice – a fresh start and a clean slate.

Afterthought

In this thumbnail sketch of you,
wearing baggy shirts and sunscreen
and talking about the war,

I've given you perhaps too many tears,
too many insufficient dreams,
too little laughter and casual sex.

I've cancelled out your joy,
you'd say, your *basso profondo*
on Tower Bridge that day,

London *flâneur*, taking photographs
of billboards, pubs and men,
a glove left on a post-box –

extravagant and glorious,
your perpetual 'and then...'

The Yard

I saw the lilac trees again —
heart-shaped leaves and long fingers
holding the summer in
as I ran below them.

War Stories

We measured out my father's homemade wine
in glasses stood together lip to lip
on the dining table – damson wine,
raisin wine and berry; my brothers called it

'rocket fuel' or 'bomber fuel' for Merlin
Rolls-Royce engines he'd worked on in the war,
Browning machineguns loaded in the wing
of a Bristol Beaufighter, his cockpit war –

picking up some requisitioned parts,
the sick pilot who'd got up from his bunk
and saw himself still on it. He'd do the parts
in different voices every Sunday lunch –

the barking drill sergeant; Colonel Uptight –
then he'd mimic smoking in the mess;
loading ammunition; abortive flights.
'The best years of your life?' I asked. 'A mess,'

he told me, 'I wouldn't wish it on a dog –
oily cylinders and sleeve valves, neglect,
senseless death, muddled orders, a dog's
breakfast, a balls up.' Or words to that effect.

Ghosts

My father always loved to tell the story
of how he once went up to Barrells Hall
on a bicycle with his eldest sister.
He had to put his hands around her waist

while she peddled her large black lady's bike
that ticked and rattled in the quiet lanes.
The sun was hot, and had been all that while,
so now a warning shimmered off the road.

He shifted to get straight but then his foot
slipped inside the spokes and tipped them off,
bloodying his knee. They walked together
up the gravel drive, the big house glowering

through the elms, then took the path that led
to the servants' quarters where a basement lounge
full of dark furniture was almost chilly
after the summer heat. My father's sister

was courting an under-butler or stable boy,
and there they were! – men with great moustaches
and oiled hair, chambermaids in aprons,
eight or so crowded round and staring.

And soon enough they talked about the ghost.
Everyone had seen her from the corner
of their eye, felt her walking up the stairs,
a chill that gave you goose pimples, or heard

footsteps in the breakfast room, the muffled
sound of weeping. Each servant had a tale
to tell of why her so unresting soul
still walked the corridors at night, what love

or desperation she must have undergone.
My father had been waiting to go out
to the privy, which always annoyed his sister
but one girl seemed to understand and said

'Now then young master, let's be having you!'
She led him down a corridor with doors
on either side with dimly shining handles.
'Do you think you can find your own way back?'

she said letting go his hand and opening
the final door. He thought he could and called out
'Thank you!' while her footsteps disappeared.
He was just about to finish when he heard

another set of footsteps coming near –
not the same ones as before, but heavier
with the rushy sound of crinolines,
a quicker foot. The door latch lifted up

and quickly, breathlessly, he said 'Hello!'
– a piping voice – just to let the lady know
and to save them both embarrassment
but she screamed the most dreadful scream

he'd ever heard, ricocheting around
the corridors, the ruined banquet hall
gutted by fire and ivy-choked, and ringing
in my father's head seventy-five years later.

Mushrooms

Apart from me, no one played the baby grand
and I only played it in order to protest.
The piano blocked the dining room – we had
to squeeze around it to feed the tinfoil barbs
I electrocuted once, clearing out the tank.
So when you came home in a hospital bed
stationed in the lounge and rigged with cot sides,
we were used to furniture that didn't fit the room:
the grandfather clock that never worked,
the dining table with an extra, central leaf.
But what took us by surprise was how you held
my mother's hands and told her that you loved her
and that as far as mushrooms went, they were
only good for being kicked down by the cows.

My Mother, Driving

My mother was never one of the avant-garde,
though she'd reverse coaches up our yard
with the best of them – 'Left hand down a bit!' –
such were the days of oil and Duraglit.

A small woman with pale and freckled arms
(five children *and* working for the coach firm)
she drove so fast, my father would have to say
'We might enjoy the countryside today

if only your mother would slow down.' The run
to Perranporth was long and through the night –
B roads, lonely windscreen-wiper sound,

with four boys in the back, an alsatian,
my sister on my father's lap. She'd wait
until he nodded off, then put her foot down.

Night Driving

Ajax lay across us or hung his head
out of the half-opened window, the car speed
pushing back his ears. And sometimes, just
to make it clear to those Cornish lanes

and high hedges, slant horizons, witches,
smugglers' tales, tin mines and lighthouse keepers,
to make it clear whose territory they were on,
he'd bark until my father said to shush,

then he'd bark again. We drove like this
as the last light gave way past Marazion
and St Michael's Mount where someone said
a giant dropped a boulder in the sea.

Our headlights shocked a pub. Towering trees
leapt in front each time we turned a bend.
We drove from petrol station to station – Shell,
Texaco, BP – their shop signs glowing

in the dark – to find the cheapest four star.
I'd been collecting petrol cards of wildlife
in 3D: dolphins jumping, chimpanzees.
Finally, when we found the cheapest,

my father must have talked about the cards
because the pump attendant said he'd sell me
a complete set – the dog let out to run
around the forecourt and pee against the sign.

The petrol booth smelt of oil and Nescafé.
He found a set of cards with a rubber band
holding them together – and there, at last,
was the aye-aye, the Magellanic penguin

and Przewalski's horse. But something deepened
in the night while my father checked the oil
and my brothers climbed back inside the car:
The Witch of Treva, carrying a hare,

The Owlman of Mawnan with staring eyes
and taloned feet, the captain who'd gone down
with his crew off White Sands Bay – all three
approached, saying now the cards were cursed.

Lanterns

The hot air balloon my brother built was made
of white crêpe paper with a balsa fireguard
to keep the flame away. It had a wire
cross and circle to hold the plug of meths-soaked
cotton-wool that Robert lit with John,
or was it Peter? lifting up the glued
and fragile corners. The flame curled violet-yellow
as the lantern filled with light. We stood
between the garage and the house, the garden
dark, the dogs locked safely in the kitchen.

My sister was very small, her face a lantern
all her own and so round that when she smiled –
she's smiling now at that angled shape of light –
her eyes closed like two crescent moons,
her Chinese Smile we called it. When Robert felt
the tug and urge to lift – our shadows like
a dial around the lawn – he let it go
to watch it fluke and wobble, then slowly rise.
His other lanterns never got off the ground,
they simply stood and burnt my mother's lawn,

but this one rose above the darkened house,
above the coaches parked up in the yard,
above St Nicholas and St John's. It rose
and drifted; guttered, dimmed, brightened again
then receded to a troubled spot of light.
My brothers had to run and give it chase
in case it came down in a farmer's field
and set the corn on fire or scared the cows.
It landed on the Mount and sputtered out.
It fell. And then my brothers brought it home.

Two Walks Home from School

Something was wrong; I knew it right away –
walking home with my junior school report
to show my mum and dad, some bad news
on the final day of term like when I stopped
at a friend of mine's to watch the wrestlers
on TV, and how I knew that it was wrong

as soon as I sat on the sofa, my body was wrong
while their muscled bodies writhed away
in front of me – blond and suntanned wrestlers
falling in a coil of arms, the school report
I carried home, not knowing why I stopped,
why time had been suspended while the news

flickered blue around me, my body's news
that made me tense and still. It wasn't wrong
for them (my friend's father always stopped
to watch the wrestling) but I couldn't turn away
while they snatched and grabbed – the smacked report
of chest on chest shouting now what wrestlers

meant to me, their writhing backs, what wrestlers
put upon a schoolboy once the news
was out and muscle had its say. The report
was news to me, as though my blood was wrong,
trembling and intense, carried away
on bruising skin and sweat and how they stopped

for a moment, clinging. My parents stopped
to open my report. I thought of wrestlers.
My father said I'd have to move away
to another school. I focused on the news
of how they forced each other down, how wrong
it was (the teachers said in my report)

that I could barely read – the worst report,
my being so far behind. The wrestlers stopped
and were made to stand apart like it was wrong –
what could my teachers say about the wrestlers?
I teemed and ached while on TV the News
showed stories where truth was turned away

like something wrong. Now my life was news –
the school report, the wrestlers' response and how,
when I walked away, I saw my future stopped.

The Fire Ritual

Take this folded manuscript and write
the names of those who loved you from the start
but mention Jane and how she walked beyond
the runner beans and lettuce to where she'd pick
the damsons while your grandma supervised.

Or after grandma died and Jane stayed on
in that draughty house across the High Street
with the alsatian she fed too many biscuits,
how she'd love to draw the parting in your hair,
dead straight, with the sharp edge of a comb.

Write about the cushion she'd have to use
to see above the steering wheel and how
she left that day to pick up Mrs Lewis
as usual from the butcher's where she worked,
a taxi job along the Stratford Road.

You knew, when you took the worried phone call —
someone asking where the taxi was,
a policeman in the yard — that nothing bad
could happen if you'd already thought it could.
The news he brought was never talked about.

So write about her here — how cold her hands were
when she woke you up for school! — then burn it
with the naming of her dog, the rug she'd thrash,
peas she'd sit and shell, her stocking-seams,
the soldier she was sweet on in the war.

Letters from Canada

I saw apple trees in the autumn foothills,
mountains out beyond and fair-haired uncles
with slurred accented speech: another life
I couldn't read on pale blue airmail paper.

I saw my father in a short-sleeved shirt,
my mother baking sponge, the boys so deep
in snow they'd have to dig their way to school!
I'd have a bedroom to myself and watch

the brighter, nearer stars – Orion, Aries,
both the silver fish. Men would be taller
and have more time, easy in themselves
without whatever we were freighted by –

inhibition, shyness, a small-town English life.
I'd get on better with my brothers then –
orchards all around us, hazelnuts and woods,
those apples heaped up in our happier arms.

Your Most Unlikely Son

Poem beginning with a line by Michael Longley

That instant I, your most unlikely son,
the youngest boy you'd never understand,
the very instant I was born, you – caught
by the camera's lens – were standing on the wing
of a Bristol Beaufighter, guiding the engine
down and thinking, in my reverie,
what you'd do once the war was over,
then fixing on the answer: wife and children.

You gave your life to coaches and Swarfega,
cricket at the weekends with Uncle Phil,
Black Rex and the publican's shy daughter.
I see you stepping in the car – my mother
stooping, pulling close her dress, a shower
of confetti, the god-almighty racket
of petrol tins and buckets when the Rover
pulled away. Soon you had three sons

climbing trees and reading war comics
but when it came to my turn, grandma said
she'd drown another boy: four years later
you finally had a girl. If no business
came knocking at your door you'd dig the garden –
a robin hopping in your clean-cut trench.
Meanwhile I grew more perplexing still,
a boy of tears I must have seemed, breaking

those chicken's eggs that day, showing off
in my tempestuous way, a 'sensitive' boy
who'd never run or make a wicket-keeper.
But as you lay dying in your hospital bed

trying to mend the broken marriages
(finding a nurse for each one of my brothers),
you called me 'Lovely in the eyes of Eve' –
your most unlikely son, your sad conundrum.

Slow Start

The coat I bought ten years ago
    became my father's coat –
    diesel fumes and wood-smoke
hung around the arms where snow

was scraped off lights. Still half awake –
    garage doors pushed open
    for coaches and the school run –
he'd pull the choke, slip the handbrake

then freewheel down the narrow yard,
    grey exhaust-smoke pluming
    bowed red brick, coiling
into itself, then up into a hard

bright day, gritted for the frost.
    The coach blocked up the High Street
    as she pulled away – the heat
just coming on, his feet at last

warming in his boots, his coat
    buttoned-up and zipped,
    his quickened sense of it;
the morning bright as May almost

and flaring in his eyes, his grandstand
    view and signalling
    to let a car pull in –
palm held up, my father's hand

like my hand from my coat, the same –
    and when I reach inside
    the pockets one last time,
they're choked with tissues, sweets and change.

And Always, Somewhere

He seemed
a deeper aspect
of the place —

the boy I'd wanted
to embrace,
his face still cut

by slanting
summer sun —
his gentle interest.

Night Chaffinch

Before the sun had left the roof,
a chaffinch settled on a twig
to sing her merry song of proof –
time and love's old whirligig.

O say you love me, say you do
and tell me how sweet time will mend
the troubled heart, the famished view
of pain and suffering without end.

The sky turned over on its side,
the common leaves were holding still.
The moon in lunar phases died
and darkness crept across the hill.

Olden Days

In the first olden days they didn't even have doors or picture frames. No one came home in a taxi or waved from a bedroom window. In the first olden days there were no chairs or coffee tables, no underwear and no light switches or bikes. But in the second olden days there were bonnets and boaters, top hats, bowler hats, porkpie hats and trilbies. Everything in the second olden days was black and white, with maybe some brown, and everyone smiled and waved flags as men in uniform left the port in boats. There wasn't a third olden days, but there were Spitfires and prime ministers, *Mellow Birds will Make you Smile*, *The Onedin Line*, milk bottles left on a doorstep with plastic covers on the top so that sparrows couldn't peck at the foil.

Balcony Scene

A man walks onto a balcony pulling out an earphone from his ear – Victorian chimneys behind him, the city sound of traffic, children playing somewhere, the sky straight out of Piero with those long, almost almond-shaped clouds, drifting slowly. 'I'm trying to be honest,' he says. 'I'm trying to stay with myself as an unhappy, depressed person.' 'A summer depression?' I ask. An airbus slowly draws a line above his head while spiders weave between the potted maple and the fig. 'I don't know if I'm staying with it or being indulgent.' 'In practice,' I say, 'it isn't easy to tell' which seems to please him but I'm thinking if I was Robert Hass, this would be a poem and I'd be writing it and now the man would have stepped inside the house again and be imagined folding his clothes.

Guide to Rain

Somewhere it's always raining – a thin, persistent rain dripping off leaves, running down tree trunks, making a gentle but weary sound like someone rustling plastic bags. Even when the sun floods the side of a building, picking up on the quality of grouting or the fixings of a gutter, when the first crocus pokes into the first spring day and down by the brook, just as years ago, a patch of snowdrops nods to the water's glint and wriggle, somewhere in a small room beyond a dark passage, it's always raining.

Settlement

We must be careful among these small paths and pine shadows. Birds skip the trees and this shingle-wind turns you all about. Gorse blocks your way. Clouds are pricked and dragged among the trees. At night what few huts there are are lit with orange light (or paler) and men walk about with torches – you can hear their boots, their breath, the rustle of their coats. Their lights are moving angles in the mist; their huts stone-built like railway arches. We must be careful of these dark mornings, these candles in a row casting yellow reflections on the parquet.

The Persian Boy

In this story, the Persian Boy is very sad – he's poor, his parents died not long after he was born. You can see him in this picture sitting on a veranda with tears running down his cheek. The sky is salmon. That's him, having to scrub floors and wash pots for his wicked uncle who has a boil on his nose. His aunt scolds him and his cousins get him blamed for everything. When he goes to market for buckwheat and pistachios, he doesn't meet a girl in falling snow. He walks home – here, you can see him – and all around the world is plum and saddle-coloured. He's so small next to the silver river and the hill. But here, in this last picture (he's on the veranda again), what's changed do you think? – the willows haven't altered, each leaf hangs exactly where we left it at the start; the persimmons are still as ripe and heavy, and the birds are just as we first encountered them, each sequestered on a branch with bronze or sea-like feathers. But there is something, don't you think? How has the artist rendered it, this new atmosphere? – as if the birds and far mountain, the trees and bright persimmons are all part of the boy's mind, or that he is a part of theirs.

Thought

A thought came to him. It seemed to mean something – like someone catching a glimpse of a bird. It came again. He thought it was the same thought as before – a worry, an idea – like a bird come back, a blackbird, or like every roof with a blackbird singing on it.

The Old Man and the Wood

An old man with cracked heels and a humped back is washing his feet in a basin at the edge of a wood. He has a kettle ready to top up the heat. The wood is dappled in a churchy gloom. Among the trees a bird is singing – it seems to be annoyed or want to give an opinion. The old man thinks it might be a scholar pedantic about his notes. And he can hear someone – Cock Robin or The Sparrow – oh far off, answering and disagreeing like a bus driver shouting to someone at the back of a bus. The man rubs his heels with pumice stone – the grey skin flakes away like dandruff or a toddler's nail clippings. He is waiting for the pink to come through.

Hero

I want to see you walk away like they do in films, backlit by city lights. I want to cry on hotel steps. I want to call your name, just once, in that broken voice I've always meant to use – you, with your blue eyes and that grin that always gets me – and have you turn around, for me to smile, do the thumbs up, then throw a bunch of keys or a torch so you can see into the labyrinth, the Minotaur's lair or just into some subway. Perhaps you'll walk away in rain or stand in rain by my graveside like they do in films. You'll be on your own holding a black umbrella after all the cars have gone. There'll be a close-up of lilies and carnations with *Always love you* written on a card. And when you turn to leave, lighting a cigarette, cupping your palms as the hero always does, your face will flush for just a moment.

Reading Cavafy

You wish you could remember an August evening
when you were twenty-one or twenty-five,
a rented room where you could hear the sea
and where the moon shone weakly through thin
and partially-opened curtains near an old taverna
or by a railway track, the hot night hushed
or noisy with tables being cleared away, revellers,
a motorino starting somewhere in an alley;
or perhaps up in an attic room above a tobacconist
at the top of a creaking stair with him asleep
on gull-white, sex-entangled sheets like a boy
from Antioch or Samothrace, his hair awry,
your love a glass set down and drained,
waiting for morning to fill it full again.

On Swanage Sands

The light against the further shore
　　　　reminds me of Vermeer –
small hotels and B&Bs,
　　　　the pier on blackened legs.

But the Punch and Judy Show
　　　　is starting up and time
does not stand still – here on the edge
　　　　of this our Golden Age,

the Professor with his megaphone
　　　　calls out the usual names:
Pretty Polly. Mr Scaramouche.
　　　　The Skeleton. Jack Ketch.

Inadequate Music

The light is lavish at the edge of day
where minor mountains shield the warming coast
and noon heat lingers in the rosemary –
a last Jerusalem, a fiery Pentecost –

while mid-air and miles away, a hawk hovers
above the setting sun and in salute
the small cicadas chirr. Warmer colours
blur like lamps in some grand institute

left burning on their stands till someone comes
and darkness is one richly darkened room
and then another – our meditations done,
our meal taken. How quietly night resumes

its tinkering with sleep, star-clad, pristine,
not bleak or monstrous, nothing we can say
in story form; the nurse will bring her morphine
as before with cocoa on a balanced tray,

a dog will bark at nothing just to hear
what nothing has to say. And so the burden
lifts, while far-off lights – tier on tier
along the bay – suggest some habitation.

Birdsong

I don't know which birds
are singing, apart from the pigeon's beat,
   but there's something sweet,
      rapid and short-lived
at home among the leaves.

I don't know whose trill
this is, this cheerful other song
   further off among
      hedges and tranquil
wooded lanes – some livelong

anthem Edward Thomas heard
between the whistling shells of France.
   Small recompense –
      a pair of blackbirds
calling from the distance,

early in black Beaurains.
But I've read the diary he wrote
   standing in his trench coat –
      snow again,
his boots already soaked,

a photograph of Helen,
continuous bombardment, shrapnel,
   roads that might hide hell
      or lead to heaven –
lark and partridge, bluebell.

A Carrot for Robert Frost

The poet was in a field pulling carrots,
the sky was grey and overcast with snow.
The poet was tugging carrots one by one –
he grasped their heads, knocking off the soil.

Most were merely carrots, merely red
but one at least would have a double root
like long men's legs amid a greener day.
And with his knife the poet made a notch,

then made another to give the man his clothes.
Most leave carrots just the way they are
but some, enraptured by the knife, will cut
a donkey where no donkey is proposed.

The Crab Mill

The yew we carved our names on by the brook –
   our Christian names, the hearts we cut,
     the arrows – were not for us

but for the girls (Judith and Alison)
   we feigned to love. The brook rolled on
     under a Midlands sun,

its moon and spit of stars. The heart you carved
   was full but mine was split in half
     while the idle waters passed.

You

I try to conjure you
by Fletcher's Ole
but there's only mud and water –
even the sheep have gone.

I wait to catch you
walking home from school
but the den below
the bridge is just a gap.

I might have seen you
coming down the path
by Station Road
but I only meet fresh air.

I'd go up to your house
but the gate is shut,
the garage closed
and all the lights are out.

In Collioure

His shield-like chest and back,
skin a perfect sand,
standing like a sailor

in the gently ebbing tide –
keep for us your pride,
your sea-wet hair

and how the sun
once drew a line around
your arms and thighs,

the angle of your jaw,
that first hot summer
in Collioure.

I Thought of Love

Today I thought of love –
it made a sighing sound
as love is wont to do,
   old or new,
tender or untrue.
Today I thought of love,
   then thought of you.

Today I thought of love
and tried to be profound
like Baudelaire or Camus –
   'Je t'aime', *'Et tu'* –
the usual ballyhoo.
Today I thought of love,
   then thought of you.

Today I thought of love
and our old stamping ground
in far off Timbuktu:
   your *'Entre Nous'* –
smiles I should have seen through.
Today I thought of love,
   then thought of you.

The Guest

Though natural beauty can't be kept
      and I can't write his name –
the shirt he wore, the tears he wept,
      his eyes a painted flame,

my knocking heart and jealousy
      a warning and a threat,
his bolstered arms, the properties
      of love that can't be met –

though age will leave his shoulder bare
      and time will touch his chest,
I'll hold his other body here
      as lover and as guest.

Winter Trees

There must be more to say of trees –
the Celtic 'calling back the sun',
the oxen bending on their knees,
the Christ Child and the Seraphim.

There must be more to say of snow
than 'all that's born must die again' –
Charon's boat, the vale of shadow,
the trial by fire or winter rain.

There must be more to say of stars
and children's blood that Herod spilt,
the Magi's journey, Lucifer
before the apple's myth of guilt.

Aaron's Brother

You'd think he was the rector by his eyes
and by the way he smiles. Let's step aside
and leave them. We have this Sunday morning ease...
Ever since he cured the bailiff's daughter
five winters back – I won't say he didn't cure her,
but who's to say, they make themselves believe –
since then they've beat a pathway to our door.
Miss Wilkes will talk the hind leg off a donkey
if you let her – they say she talked her husband
half to death. I know a shortcut out
across the fields, a pretty way and quieter
without the likes of her; I'll guarantee
there's time enough to stay awhile and talk.
The ladies like to have him to themselves,
you wouldn't get a word in. I didn't catch
your name....

      We can sit here on this gravestone –
the dead can't mind, there's no offence to God.
Doubtless you've been sent to seek him out?
Men like you come from miles around
to open out their fears – I hear them murmur
through the kitchen door, young men mostly
like yourself. He listens right enough,
I'll give him that, but something in his bearing
makes me small, so that folk almost wonder
who I am. Oh, I can spin a yarn
as good as any, better some would say,
but I can see they'd rather it be him.

Just the other day he came in dusty
from the yard and made one of his *pronouncements* –
contradicted me in front of everyone,

made me feel a proper fool, and I'm supposed
to shrug it off and take it in my stride?
Go out cheerful now in the low pasture?
They'll take his word on everything – the tides,
the cider crop, how to fix a plough
or bring up children – not that he's got children
of his own, nor never looked to have them,
I can tell you! 'He's worth his weight in gold'
they'll say, but I'm the one who has to scrimp
and get things in and haggle over prices
with pigs to feed and fifty laying hens.

Just the other day I caught him praying
in the yard without his hat – a bucket
of potato peelings left idle by his side,
the usual blur of glory in his eyes,
his voice so low and quiet I had to stop
what I was doing just to hear him out.
He's taken to praying like that in the shop.
He'll go down on his knees among the sacks
without a thought to customers about.
The rector turns his back but the ladies
hang on every word – 'You must be proud
to have a brother who speaks to God like that.'
They'll call out for a chair and tot of brandy.

There was a time when we were more than brothers,
before the prayers and shivering took him, when father
had to run the shop and keep the farm.
We'd have to fetch and carry – loaves and such –
and being only boys, and me the eldest,
father told me I should hold his hand;
so falling to a quieter stride, we dallied,
filling up the time with tales of knights
and dragons' dens, and women pure as coin.
Sometimes I would take the lead but mostly

Aaron with fantastic talk would soar
beyond our mortal ken, mixed up with what
we saw in passing – a parliament of rooks,
a hare dodging in a field of grazing sheep.
We'd walk past Mrs Wilson's house, her shadow
at the window keeping watch, and oftentimes
Sire Jenkins on Old Roy, pulling the reins
while that stubborn horse ate clover by the roadside
and only trotted on when he was ready.
Aaron loved that horse – he'd stroke and whisper
but the beast would turn his head away as if
he'd seen a heaven beyond our human sight.

Two Celtic crosses grace this little churchyard
and if you like I'll show you where they are.
You needn't worry – they've a long and halting walk
with old Miss Jenkins hampering their stride.
I've had my visions, if it's them you've come about?
Once, when the rain came sudden down, we sheltered
under an oak and talked about the war
between the angels and how God had thrown
Lucifer into the fiery pit forever.
Darkness gathered round about our words
and hid our fearful faces while pelting rain
made a great cathedral of sound. I fainted –
the earth rushed up and blocked my eyes and mouth.
I dreamt a host of demons snatched my arms
and grasped my slippy ankles but then a figure,
arrayed in dazzling light, took my hand
and showed me to Jerusalem with angels
back and forth and walls of beaten bronze
set about with pearls and flowery garlands –
no earthly tongue could tell you what I saw.
I asked my guide what it betokened, this fair
and pleasant mount with gates and olive trees,
but when he turned I woke up in my bed

with Aaron slumped and sleeping in a chair.
I reached to touch his hair – he called out *father!*
and all the house was noise.

                        A blackbird – listen! –
one of the three birds of Rhiannon, singing
the dead to life or lulling us to sleep...
They told me I'd been to the brink of death,
how Aaron blamed himself and couldn't rest
for watching at my side. They fetched the rector.
I talked about the winding thorny way,
the blessèd angels ascending and descending
but he wanted me to stop. We prayed together
and soon enough I gained my health and strength.
Well, my vision didn't stay and Aaron,
he fell into a sickness not long after.
He took to walking out, friendless and fretful,
blaming himself for what had befallen me.
One night the house was woken up with shouts
and swinging lamps. I fumbled with the latch –
the horses' hooves were gunshot in the yard,
a body lifted – but father sent me back.
That's when Aaron's visitations started,
along with fever sweats and bed wetting.
You're anxious, I can tell, to join your friends
but if you keep an eye on where the lane
appears, there, behind that hazel copse,
we'll meet them in the parlour when they come.

After father died, after we had put him
in the earth a winter's morning – the ground
so hard the diggers had to use a pick –
my aunt was called to keep the house while I
was always busy in the shop. One night –
I'd gone out back to sort the takings – Aaron
came in out of breath and babbling, saying

he'd seen a man beside the damson tree,
a man of smoke, with hands in supplication.
I tried to calm his nerves but then he screamed
and rolled his eyes and talked to empty space.
No one wanted him to lift a finger
after that, so he did his sums and schooling
here at home, lying in his bed and writing
'sayings' in the margins of a Bible.

Help me up. My legs aren't young as yours.
Don't worry we can keep the road in sight.
I'll show you to those crosses. There'll be others...
I'd say he took my visions on himself,
wouldn't you? I'm half afraid to think it.
Let's enjoy this festival of sun...
There'll be others gathered hanging on his words,
making that recognition-sound each time
his voice dips and darkens and he gestures
– like this – as if he held an apple up.
He'll say he knows the answer to your thoughts,
or that one thought forming in your mind –
some nicety of God. But I know better.
I've seen him when he readies himself for church,
standing at the oval mirror in the hall
combing his hair, smoothing it down, then settling
and resetting that old grey shawl of his.
You should see the way he eats, mopping up
his gravy with a balled-up pinch of bread!

Would you take my arm? The ground is soft
and molehills... That's better. It's not that we don't talk.
He'll follow while I'm shutting up the shop,
slowing down my work, asking about
some ragamuffin he's set his sights on helping.
Sometimes, when I'm putting out the eggs,
he'll take the broom away and call me brother –

even sometimes with a tear in his eye!
I've seen him touch a young man's face; I've seen
the youngster blush, then leave off what he planned.
(Just between ourselves, he'll take half
a glass of sherry after Sunday lunch.)
My mother's grave is hereabouts; she died
when we were small; wouldn't have a headstone –
said we shouldn't need one to remember.

A lad like you, with a goodly head of hair –
just a lick of auburn peeping through –
you can rest assured he'll want to ask you back.
On evening walks or idle morning strolls
to Wideacres or past Pennycrocker Farm,
he'll tell you just how close you are to God.
You'll be basking in the blessing of his looks
and in his loving words but then he'll cool
and some scruffy farmer's boy or ne'er-do-well
will catch his violent interest for a while
and you'll be back among the lookers-on.

We'll meet them soon enough – each time he talks
he has this way of stopping, however far
you need to go. Here's the oldest cross,
brought from where it marked the pilgrim's route
or where you'd ford a stream. You'll forgive me
if we sit here on this bench and take the view?
Just let me catch my breath. Sit a moment...
When you close your eyes, do you meet our Lord?
And does He speak, and do you give Him thanks?
There's just a darkness turning in my head
and when I pray I think of cormorants
diving for their catch and how the impact
slowly blinds them.

                    I see you're well brought up –

judging by the fashion of your jacket
and your polished Sunday boots. Perhaps
you have a younger brother of your own?
The likes of you can't be spared this time of year,
so I daresay someone's sweating for your ease.
Don't start. I mean no offence, but someone
should know the truth, a God-fearing man like you,
a nip of truth won't hurt, seeing as you've
laboured all this way to hear some preaching –
'How gently our prayers should reach the ear of God.'
And don't be thinking 'sights', I leave all that
to Aaron along with dreams and prophecies –
a branch that turns into a snake, a bird...

My truth is closer; you'll think it devil's work.
I'm not his mother's son and not his father's.
I was the Prichards' boy; youngest of eight –
I never knew them. Mrs Prichard took pity
on my mother, seeing as how she couldn't
be having children, or so the story goes –
they were poor as church mice. They gave me up,
grateful, I shouldn't wonder, to have one less
mouth to feed. A kindness do you think?
They moved away and our families lost touch.
Then Aaron came, a blessing at her age,
and we grew up as brothers and more than brothers.
Don't look away – I see you catch my drift.
'Their blood shall be upon them' the Bible says.
I was standing by the fire in our tin bath,
getting the pleasure of it, my feet still soaking,
when I felt that someone watched, you know
like how you feel a ghost – I was twelve
or thereabouts. I turned to look and there
was Aaron stood inside the fire's glow.
The flames were hot. The embers cracked and fell.
I thought he'd look away for shame but then

he motioned with his hand to turn around.
You've been silent all this while but now
I see you blushing among the fiends of hell.

Let's say we've spent an hour in contemplation
of his love but when you set him down
as fair or foul or common herring, remember
he's a better man than you and all your kind –
'The Lord sent his lions amongst them to slay them...'
A bit of spit and polish to ease your conscience,
that's all it is, a rose of aspiration
to pin on your lapel. You won't change,
he knows that (despite your bandied scripture),
but he'll like those eyes you've got, blueness,
he'll like that, and no doubt you hope to ask
that clever question you've stored up in your heart.
Cat got your tongue? You've not read your Isaiah,
'Even the young shall faint and grow weary.'
You'll be thinking almonds from Aaron's rod
that blossomed to proclaim the Holy choice –
strange fruit to ripen on a withered stick.

And all this time that blackbird sings as if
nothing were amiss – a little love song
just for our amusement, yours and mine.
And just as I predicted, here they come,
you can see them, there, men and women
who hardly seem to move. How small they look!
We understand each other now I think
and I know that I can bank upon your silence.
We've time before they get back to the house –
they've a hymn to sing and prayers before
they settle down to talk – so what say you
I show you round the church? 'A dram of sweet
is worth a pound of sour' the saying goes.
The door is open to those who seek Him out

and there's still the gentle breath of God
calming the perturbations of our soul.
You'll be used to grander sights, I'll warrant,
but the font you'll find, is worth the time of day
and our handsome new east window, paid for
by parishioners' donations, depicts Christ
as the Good Shepherd watching o'er His flock.

Owl Night

All day the wind has ranged across
the valley – it gave the pines their hour,
thrashed their branches, milled their tops

but now the limestone ridge is scoured
into a milky non-existence.
The day is sealed; the mountains tower

beyond the pale, deleted distance.
You can hear the birds' arcade,
the wind undoing its persistence.

Nature's apple colours fade.
I wash my cup and scrub a saucepan,
then go to bed. The debt is paid –

consciousness is overrun.
The owl's one hoot tells night to come.

NOTES

'The Cattle Farmer's Tale' (16) was inspired by the Dhaniya Sutta from the Sutta Nipata – a collection of discourses containing some of the earliest Buddhist teaching. The poem contains direct translation as well as material from other Buddhist sources, especially the *Dhammapada*. Although I've followed the sense of the sutta, I wouldn't call it a "translation" or even a "version", more like a poem "inspired by" the sutta. Note: *kummasa* is a very poor food made of what we would call mung beans.

'*from* The Daybook of Li Shu Tong' (26) purports to be a translation of a daybook written by the Chinese painter, poet and monk, Hong Yi (1880–1942). It isn't. 'Dajian' is the posthumous name of Huineng, traditionally seen as the Sixth and last Patriarch of Chán Buddhism.

'Two Birds for Kabir' (39) began as a result of watching a documentary about Kabir, the Indian mystic poet and saint *(c.*1440 – *c.*1518). I was especially struck by the raga, 'There is a strange tree, which stands without roots and bears fruits without blossoming...'

'The Travellers from Orissa' (40). According to tradition, Tapussa and Bhallika were the first disciples of the Buddha. The story goes that they met the Buddha not long after his Enlightenment at Uruvela (the original name of Bodh Gaya). They gave the Buddha his first meal – barley gruel and honey balls. After that they pretty much disappear from Buddhist literature. I was fascinated to learn that there are still areas of Orissa today where people still consider themselves Buddhists; so the story may well contain a kernel of truth.

'A Carrot for Robert Frost' (93) is based on a metaphor Frost used in 'Remarks on Form in Poetry' (*The Collected Prose of Robert Frost*. New York, Library of America, p. 79).